PMP Memory Guide
A Short and Sweet Pocket Book
Robert Keller, MBA

Other books by Robert Keller

Only Bees Die: Peace Corps Eastern Europe

INDEX

PURPOSE & EXPLANATION

This guide by itself is not enough to pass the PMP. Nor is it meant to be. Its purpose is to simply provide easy methods for people to create their own supplemental memory aids in conjunction with their own study habits and material. As such, I do not dive into explanations and definitions of common PMP terms and acronyms. It's subtitled "short and sweet" for a reason.

My memorization approach evolved because as a kid I used to have trouble remembering key items from middle school in order to do my homework. To solve this little problem my mom dumped me in an afterschool study group that gave me a fundamental tool for success: get over the concept of remembering everything perfectly all the time; most kids are not savants and should not try to be. Instead, realize that your brain is always recording your life—like when you randomly remember something insignificant from childhood—and start imprinting "triggers" into your life to be able to access those memories. A basic association technique to link memories together. One trick to this is an easy doodle or simple drawing (appealing to me since I'm a visual learner), which is mostly what this guide is about. If the discussion was about water pollution, I drew a sick fish. If there were three key points the teacher noted I didn't try to precisely copy each one down. Instead I drew three gills, or three fins, or three bubbles to remind myself that there were three *somethings*. Then I just associated each s*omething* with a single word or simple phrase. For example, the Scope Baseline contains the Scope Statement, the Work Breakdown Structure, and the Work Breakdown Structure Dictionary. Or, more simply, the SBL = SS + WBS + WBSDic. If you keep breaking it down and refining a memory path by continually reviewing it, eventually all you need is very basic trigger, SBL = 3.

Overall I came out of that class with the mantra "simplify and link" on my brain. Just…keep it simple.

Which is what I tried to do with the PMP. I passed at any rate, so I must have done something right.

Before actually diving into the test, but after I was seated with my scratch paper, I took me about 10 minutes to recall and draw up these few aids from memory. I used the full front and back of one page of 8.5 by 11 inch paper, leaving plenty of room for notations. These are *my* simple memory triggers and are just examples for you to use to build your own. In case you're well on your way to the PMP, I'll present my cheat sheet by itself first, and then dive into explaining each one. Stop reading whenever you feel you know enough to pass.

A:

	I	P	E	MC	C
I	Develop Charter	DPMP	DMPE *defects*	MCPW ICC	P & P
S		Collect Req Define Scope Create WBS		Verify Control	
T		Define Act *Activity List* Sequence Acts Est Act Resources Est Act Durations Develop Schedule		Control Schedule	
Cost		Est Cost Det Budget			
Q			Perform QA	Perform QC	
HR		*Staffing mgnt plan*	Acquire Team Develop Team Manage Team		
Comm	ID Stakes		Dist Info Manage Stakes	Report Performance	
R		Plan RM ID Risks *Risk List* Perform Qual Perform Quan Risk Response			
P		Plan P	Administer P *Bidder Conf Select Sellers*	Conduct P	Close P

B:

FP	FFP details known
	FPIF Incentive
	FP EPA many years
CR	CRFF fixed fee
	CRAF Award
	CP%C
T&M	unknown $, unknown finish

C:

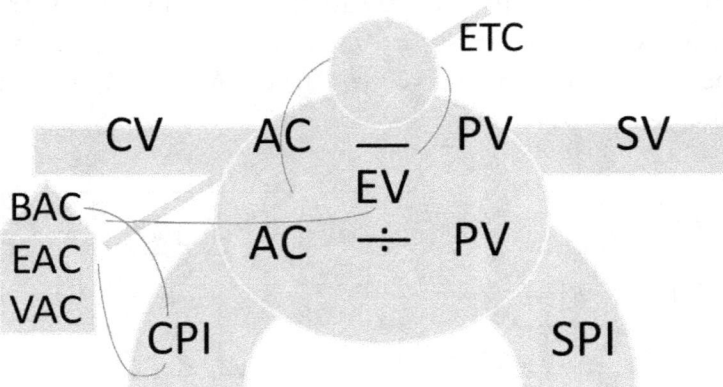

ETC

CV AC — PV SV
          EV
BAC
EAC AC ÷ PV
VAC
     CPI   SPI

D:

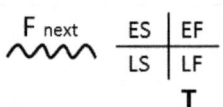

F next	ES	EF
	LS	LF

T

E:

FWD	ES		-1	EF
BKD	LF	D	+1	LS

F:

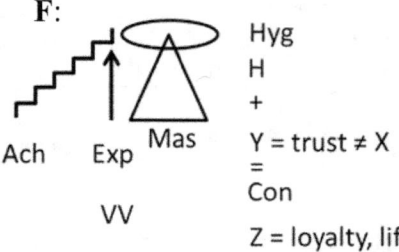

Ach   Exp   Mas

VV

Hyg
H
+
Y = trust ≠ X
=
Con
Z = loyalty, life

G:

C	0	
D	85	
J	detect	
F	TQM f	
S	TCM gf	Control
		P D ✓ A

That's it, just these six things, all drawn by memory. We are not talking brain surgery here.

A: Process Groups and Knowledge Areas

	I	P	E	MC	C
I	Develop Charter	DPMP	DMPE *defects*	MCPW ICC	P & P
S		Collect Req Define Scope Create WBS		Verify Control	
T		Define Act *Activity List* Sequence Acts Est Act Resources Est Act Durations Develop Schedule		Control Schedule	
Cost		Est Cost Det Budget			
Q			Perform QA	Perform QC	
HR		*Staffing mgnt plan*	Acquire Team Develop Team Manage Team		
Comm	ID Stakes		Dist Info Manage Stakes	Report Performance	
R		Plan RM ID Risks *Risk List* Perform Qual Perform Quan Risk Response			
P		Plan P	Administer P *Bidder Conf* *Select Sellers*	Conduct P	Close P

Ah, the framework of the whole thing. Once you dive into all the PMP material, you'll start to see all sorts of process maps and linkages between tools and techniques shared across disciplines plus other confusing, big, colorful messes about how the PMP exam covers both process groups and knowledge areas and how they overlap and intertwine. Maybe those things work for other people. I dunno; for me, they did not, and they cluttered my brain, so I built my own to simplify things. That's this grid.

To start establishing memory links, just notice little things. Like, that it's 10 x 6 squares. If you look at it right, there is kind of a *Figure 8* in the middle. Also note how many white squares there are; it's a grid yes, but not every square is filled to the brim with information. These types of little self-notes will help you remember stuff. While taking the test you very well may experience mental blocks: you know you studied *something*, you know you know the answer, but you can't quite recall it. Little things like a *Figure 8* in a 10 x 6 grid might be enough to jog your memory so you can fill in the gaps.

Across the top row are the process groups: Initiating, Planning, Executing, Monitoring and Controlling, and Closing. I remember them as a simple lyric of their first letters that sounds like "I pee and eee, em see and see." Down the left-hand side in the first column are the knowledge areas. They each share the same entry and exit word, Project and Management, so no need to remember that. Just the middle word. So Project Integration Management is just "Integration" or as I have it: *I*. Going straight down from there the others stand for: Scope, Time, Cost, Quality, Human Resources, Communications, Risk, and Procurement. I tried to make up a similar lyric and failed, I tried a sentence and failed, and eventually after writing it down several times I ended up just memorizing it the old fashioned way. So whatever works for you, go for it.

Now, the inside stuff. All the regular text denotes a PMP process. These are just my shorthand forms for them. The more you study the more this will crystalize, so I'll skip explaining each one; that's what they are, and they don't change no matter how they're visualized. The *italicized* words though, those are my biggies. In various different tests I noticed those things were always asked about. There are lots and lots of inputs, outputs, tools, and techniques (ITTO as they're collectively called) in the Project Procurement Management Knowledge Area for instance, but repeatedly I found that there were numerous questions on every test about both *bidder conferences* and *select sellers*, so those things I added to the matrix to remember in what process and knowledge area they fit. Those two, along with the *staffing management plan*, *activity list*, and *defects* were my five target study areas of all the ITTOs of all the processes. And there are like 500 in total! I didn't even try to memorize them all. Instead I just targeted what I noticed kept coming up in the practice tests.

Now, to me, all of that is a pretty sound approach. The exam is predicated on being respected and useful, so of course the lion's share of the questions will be devoted to questions that cover topics applicable to all industries: contracts, staffing, finding and fixing problems, etc. This is the main reason why you should be taking practice tests from all over: the more you take the more you see what everybody else thinks are the important areas of project management. Maybe you'll get stuck on a few questions that require deep-knowledge understanding, but if you've prepared yourself for the *most likely* questions, you'll pass. And that—after all is said and done—is the point.

My first choice to remember something is alphabetical. So for the HR row in the E column, Acquire is before Develop and Manage is last. ADM is the trigger. Same for Risks, Qualitative comes before Quantitative. As you study what's in each process it becomes more and more important to just know the trigger to order your memories and avoid being confused. You'll consume a lot of information gearing up for the PMP. The trick is orderly access to what you've seen and studied, not just rote memorization. If alphabetizing a list won't work, try it backwards. Just the fact that it's backwards is often enough to remember it: you have to Estimate Costs before you can Develop Budget for instance.

My second choice for memorization is a sequence that sounds like an action. DSEED sounds like an actual word and that's all it took to take root in my mind and remember the order of the processes contained in the Time Management (row T) and Planning (column P) intersection.

Play with the grid a little to familiarize yourself with it. Take notes in it. "Hey, look at that, most of the processes are in the Planning column. Okay, which ones aren't then?" Get used to writing it out from memory for each practice test you take; don't use the same sheet. Establish your own links and synapses based on what you see and think.

B: Contract Types

FP	FFP details known	
	FPIF Incentive	
	FP EPA many years	
CR	CRFF fixed fee	
	CRAF Award	
	CP%C	
T&M	unknown $, unknown finish	

This one is all about contracts. There are three types: fixed-price, cost-reimbursable, and time and materials. The first two have subcategories: firm fixed-price, fixed-price with an incentive fee, and fixed-price with economic price adjustment; cost-reimbursable with fixed fee, cost-reimbursable with award fee, and cost-reimbursable with percentage of cost. There are differences between each, including reasons why you would choose one over another, but the main thing for the test is identifying which is which. You're not a contracting officer; you just need enough information to ballpark it. For instance, what is the difference between an Award and an Incentive? If you reach a target you receive an incentive fee; it's out of the subjective realm. Hard logic rules that roost. Either you hit a target (45% done by January 31st, as measured by blah, blah, blah) or you don't. An award however, is all subjective. The buyer gives you the contract for the amount negotiated and if you "do a solid, bang up job" the buyer reserves the right to tack on something extra. It's subjective. There is more to it than that, lots of underlying explanations and ins and outs associated with them, but for the test you just need to know enough to make the call between a multiple choice list. "What are the key differences?" That's the question.

No fancy tricks on this one. I just continually wrote it down to memorize it. The memory keys are just the words associated with each. "When would you choose a time and materials contract?" Why, when it's unknown exactly what you want to build, or how long it will take, or both. Unknown money ($) and unknown finish (date) indicate a T&M.

C: Phat Man Phishing

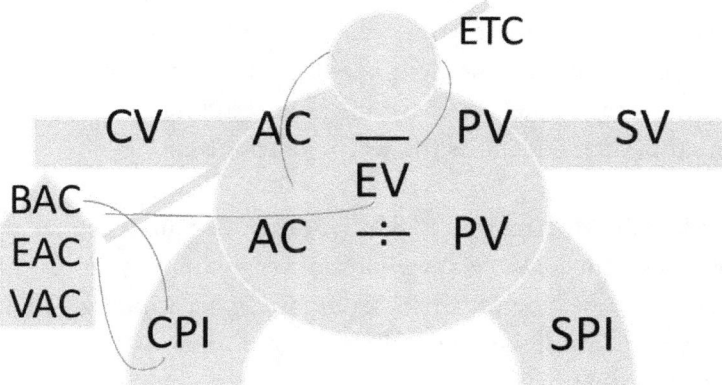

This is actually the first drawing I formalized to help me pass the exam. I was working with the Earned Value equations trying to find a way to link relationships when I hit on this guy. To draw him I start with EV in the center, since that's the most common variable in these equations. Moving *up* from there, either subtracting AC or PV gives you a variance (CV and SV, respectively). Moving *down* the same way yields a performance index. If you think left-to-right, it's easy alphabetical memorization for the basics: A is before P. If you think logically, subtraction is easier than division, so it "floats" to the top. His gut has the calculations, his feet and hands the final products. Playing with the location of the variables I added the BAC "tackle box" (note that it's also alphabetical: B, E, V). BAC + EAC = VAC. Then the "fishing pole" to point to ETC. EAC − AC = ETC. Yup, awesome.

But there's more! Starting with BAC, there are two more fun equations if you follow the "fishing lines." BAC divided by CPI is EAC in most cases, that's the little loop around his left foot. The next most common instance to find EAC (in my opinion) is AC + BAC − EV, which is the loop around his neck. If I can't remember the exact equation then I at least want to remember how to find the equation and what variables are involved. If push comes to shove on the exam at least you can increase your odds by eliminating choices you know don't contain the right variables. Play with this diagram a little, draw your own fishing lines and tackle boxes to remember the equations the way you want to.

Incidentally, for myself I didn't bother explaining what the variables actually *mean* anywhere in my own study notes. No need. The questions themselves itemize what is being sought, so even without knowing their definitions you can usually solve for them. If you do happen to get one asking about knowledge, here's a tip: if the choice is between money and schedule for which is more important, money wins. Same as in real life. It's alright if something is a little bit late, but if that same something is done on time but at a higher cost, you'll hear about it from upper management. It's easier to wait than to open your wallet.

D: Critical Path #1

$$\overset{\text{F next}}{\wedge\wedge\wedge} \quad \begin{array}{c|c} \text{ES} & \text{EF} \\ \hline \text{LS} & \text{LF} \end{array}$$

$$\mathbf{T}$$

Get ready for simplicity because this diagram is all about remembering Free Float and Total Float. Free Float is used when you're talking about delaying the next activity in line. Total Float is the same discussion, except it's about affecting the end of the project. For this diagram, the F on the left is read along the top with the ES and EF, since that's how Free Float is calculated: ES and EF of the next activity in the sequence. And what floats freely? Ducks, boats, whatever you want the answer to be. For me it's a submarine. Ultimately it doesn't matter, just that those waves remind me of the term "floats freely." Total Float is found by subtracting EF from LF, that's where the T comes in at the lower right. I start there and read up to remind myself of the equation.

E: Critical Path #2

FWD	ES	D	-1	EF
BKD	LF		+1	LS

Now here we're talking about Forward and Backward Passes, and this is the simplest I could make the trigger. FWD = ES + Duration − 1 = EF. BKD = LF − Duration + 1 = LS. Nothing grand, nothing exciting, just a box diagram placeholder for my mind until I come upon a question where I need to remember those pieces and how they fit together.

Notice that if you were to fold the Free Float/Total Float diagram over this one, the last column here matches the first column there. That trick also helped me: I always draw these two right next to each other.

F: Motivational Theories

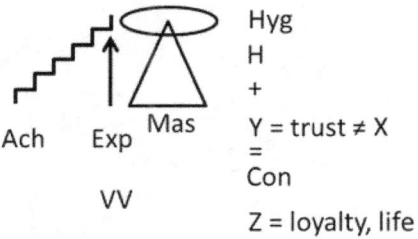

Hyg
H
+
Y = trust ≠ X
=
Con

Z = loyalty, life

Ach   Exp   Mas

VV

I almost didn't include this one because I only had three questions about motivational theory and theorists. A whopping 1.5%. Still, this technique is easy to use and the diagram easy to remember so I decided to keep it. The pyramid is Maslow's Hierarchy of Needs, which most people have heard of. That's where I start when I draw this. The halo at the top represents hygiene factors because they are things at work affecting you from outside, so the circle is like inner peace, which is sorta Herzberg's theory (hence the Hyg and the H right under it). Achievement Theory is represented by the steps and Expectancy Theory by the arrow. The difference is that *achievement*, to me, seems more likely that you'll get somewhere if you do the work of climbing the staircase. Expectancy Theory questions all seemed to be built on a reward system where the key thing was a worker looking to the payoff (or "up" at it, as represented by the arrow) and determining it's real worth. Again, these are my triggers to access my thoughts about all the reading and practice questions I have stored in my brain. Who came up with Expectancy? Victor Vroom (VV). *Vroom, vroom!* The noise and engine makes when it revs up, getting louder, increasing. Another arrow association in my mind. Contingency Theory is confusing to me, but I realize it's like a hybrid of Hygiene and Theory Y, or, reading down: Hyg + Y = Con. Theory Y and Theory Z are pretty easy to remember. I think of them in relation to trust of employees, Y has it, X doesn't. Theory Z typically has two associated words within any question about it: *loyalty* and *life or lifetime*.

G: Quality Kingpins

C	0	
D	85	
J	detect	
F	TQM f	
S	TCM gf	Control
		P D ✓A

Again, I hesitate. But this one is probably the easiest of the bunch. Here's what it says: Crosby = zero defects. Deming = 85% of cost of quality is directly linked to management. Juran = detecting processes that are out of control. Alphabetized: C, D, J! 0 comes before 85, and numbers before letters! These three are the top dogs of quality management theory as we know it today. However, their work was itself built on that of two other gentlemen. Feigenbaum = father of Total Quality Management. Shewhart = Total Control Methodology, in fact, probably the grandfather of the entire quality management idea, and he first came up with Plan Do Check Act.

Is there a lot more to quality management principles and theories? Yes. Will any of it be on the test? Probably not. It wasn't on mine. I honestly don't remember *any* questions about these guys. But I do remember lots of practice questions that could be answered just by knowing the key words associated with the names in the paragraph above, which is how the chart came to be. Better to have it and not need it I suppose.

EXAM THOUGHTS

So after spewing out these memory triggers, how did I do on the exam and what was it like? I passed obviously, but it took me the full four hours to finish and I was dead last to leave the room. Hell, it took me about two hours just to get through one pass of all 200 questions, marking questions I wasn't sure of right off the bat plus any I didn't want to calculate out. That's two hours just to read every question and answer maybe 15% or so just because they were gimmes. In my opinion, that percentage, although totally a rough estimate, is useful because according to everything I read and absorbed on internet forums and blogs, you're shooting for a 65% to pass. So start adding your strengths up and nailing down questions that are clearly going to be on the test: anything to calculate (Earned Value, leads and lags, critical path stuff), all the contracts stuff, anything to do with legal ramifications, getting scheduling in order, stakeholder management and communication, and project scope are my personal recommendations. Those are the things that have the most real-world value and are therefore the things that transcend industry bounds. Other stuff, like historical information on who is the father of what motivational theory *might* come up; but that list of subjects *should* come up. My guess is that being knowledgeable about just those topics probably edges a person pretty darn close to the 50% mark, and with another round of 15% of easy ones like I experienced, you're probably looking at passing.

The remaining 35% is made up of a host of various questions. My analogy is that the PMP is like a forest of a thousand trees with several paths through it. Your job is to get to the other side. You can make use of as many paths as you can, but no path is a straight shot through to the end. So any of those thousand trees *might* be on the test, but only a fool would forge ahead through the heavy brush when there is a path right there for the taking.

After the first two hours I took a break for five minutes or so to just wander around. In my test center the rules were pretty strict: you could go to a bathroom on that floor of the building but not anywhere else, up or down. You could not go to your locker to look at notes. You had to empty your pockets of everything except your locker key to get back into the exam room, and they visually and electronically checked you for any deviations from those rules. It was like airport security. The next 75 minutes or so I spent doing the questions I had marked for calculations and that were in the category of "I probably know this, but I'll need to reason it out." I again skipped the ones that I just did not know. Time was a constraint and I felt myself backing up against that wall. Another break to clear my head and then I sprinted the last 30 to 40 minutes to try my luck at those questions I was just clueless on.

It is worth a paragraph to verbally abuse people who don't realize the etiquette of these types of tests, tests taken in a room full of other people, all thinking hard, all in their own world, taking their own tests. Like the two people in my test center. The guy behind me had the headphones on and probably didn't realize he was turbo-tapping his foot on his chair. Loudly. He noticed the stink-eye me and another dude laid on him though. *Knock that off. We're concentrating here.* Later on, the woman behind me started talking to herself, saying her questions out loud. Yeah, really. Dead silence in the room, everyone engrossed in their own thing, then her whisper, crashing through the silence like a raging monkey in the jungle. So keep your calm and keep your quiet and be courteous to other testers.

Personally, my theory is that over the last decade the PMP certification has gone through some serious changes. When it first came out it was fairly straightforward and people just took a regular multiple choice test with one clear right answer according to PMI standards; a high school test. But that was too easy and they revised it to a more conceptual approach and people needed a stronger background in logical reasoning and test taking. More like a college exam: if you rushed through it you would make simple mistakes; it became more of a brain teaser sort of thing. But that wasn't quite right either. Now, it's becoming more executive-level with "why?" questions.

For instance, consider this:

A project manager of a culturally diverse team located in 3 geographical areas in 2 different countries (non-adjacent) with total team membership of 27 employees under her leadership has a problem. Within the next month a Quality Assurance team is joining the project and an existing team is closing its office in one region. The new team consists of 9 people and the closing office consists of 13 current employees who are being reassigned to new projects.

Why is it important for a project manager to understand communication channels?

a) Because the Plan Communication process determines who gets what when and in what format.
b) Because the Communications. Requirements Analysis technique includes analyzing and determining the needs of stakeholders and houses the Communication Channels and lines of communication diagram method.

c) Because the project manager must distribute information both vertically and horizontally depending on the needs of the receiver.
d) Because communication is what project managers spend most of their time doing and the more is understood about how it works, the better.

Yeah, BAM! In your face! *All* of those answers are true and *none* are a good answer to the question being asked. If I had to guess I'd go with D, but even if that's right, so what? What's the real use of *any* of those answers? Who cares how many communication channels there are as long as you are, in fact, communicating? Knowing all the channels is way less important than knowing the actual people you need to establish communications with. It's these types of criticisms that are changing the test. On the plus side, this is actually pretty real-world representative; I've certainly been in meetings where justification is needed verbally and if the PM can't deliver a convincing argument to a short question the project is sunk. But for a test I prefer something a little more obvious where I can whittle away the wrong answers. This is just an example of the curve balls you'll be thrown on the exam. Best preparation is to learn the foundational stuff and just breathe deeply, consider all the options, and work your way up from the least useful answer to the most relevant one, even if it's not a perfect hole-in-one.

Note the key thing here: the PMP is a living test. It's revised every few years. There is a whole industry around test preparation, test skills, sample exams, you name it. Those companies are not going to let that cash cow go out to pasture to die easily; they're gonna milk it. When you're checking out books from the library note the latest copyright dates of the material. The closer it is to the present the better it is. I found calling PMI and talking to their operators to be helpful as well. They gave me advice on when the next change to the exam was coming so I knew the best bet for me was to study with material available now and take it before the next update happened.

APPROACH

In case you care, an annotated outline on how I passed:

1. Poked around online before I paid for anything to get a sense of what's what with this thing.
   a. A lot people noted intense study times: several hours each day for several weeks.
   b. Bookmarked the free exams online that seemed the most useful. There are a ton.
   c. If you don't take practice exams, you're sunk. This guide is not enough for you to pass; it's only a way to organize your approach.
2. Visited the PMI website to register.
3. Checked out various books from the library.
   a. I used three: *PMP: Project Management Professional Exam Study Guide* by Kim Heldman, 6th edition, 2011; *Head First PMP* by Jennifer Greene and Andrew Stellman, 2nd edition, 2009; *The PMP Exam: How to Pass on Your First Try* by Andy Crowe, 2nd edition, 2005.
   b. In order of me using them: *Head First* breaks it down with great analogies to simply explain the core concepts. Unfortunately, it's too simple and that 2nd edition was way too elementary and out of date compared to my exam. *How to Pass* was good with more questions and a better sample test selection, but even farther out of date. *Study Guide* was the most in-depth and is daunting at first, but her questions are the closest to the test.
   c. Took an Assessment Test of 75 questions to see what I knew, what I didn't, and what areas I should target. I scored a 50%, or put

another way, all I needed to learn was a minimum of 15% more stuff to pass.

    d. **This is the first key concept: the test is pass/fail,** so concentrate on what you think the exam will mostly be about, based on your research. Do not focus on very rare questions.

    e. If I were to do it again I would stick to Heldman's *Study Guide* only. Best prep questions and her format highlights in boxes stuff to target for the exam. Downside is she includes asides and discusses things relevant to project management life outside of the exam. While interesting, I'm here for the exam, and the exam only.

    f. I didn't read any of these books cover to cover. I skimmed each chapter for bold and italicized text to get an idea what it talked about, took the standard end of chapter practice tests to familiarize myself with the questions and content, and then targeted those areas that I missed. I don't use a holistic approach, I use surgical. But that's me.

4. Registered via PMI website for my local test center and paid the second part of the fee.

    a. **Second key concept:** Realized I could "brain dump" my noodle onto the scratch paper before ever reading an exam question and thereby arm myself before the battle.

5. Established the habit of taking mini tests every day of 20 to 30 questions.

    a. **Third key concept:** I noticed that if I missed a few days for whatever reason I fell out of the zone and would miss the same questions again, even though I had reviewed them. Better to stay solidly in test taking mode.

b. To establish the memory triggers and draw diagrams I jotted down notes and repeat concepts that I missed.

c. Began drawing from memory my diagrams and notes to beef up the synapses. I did this whenever I could: waiting at the dentist, in between meetings, watching TV, etc.

d. Took a lot of sample internet prep exams. There is a wide variety available but it helped me to use that variety just to sharpen my skills. Plus, I could sneak in a quick set of questions throughout the day. Just because I started a 50 question test didn't mean I had to finish it. Tests that don't require you to finish before showing you the correct answer are particularly useful.

6. Exam day I went to the library first to prepare.

a. Spent a few hours there, away from house and work, free of distractions, to just be in the zone of taking the test.

b. Reviewed my notes pages right in the car in the parking garage to prep myself for the brain dump I would make in the very near future.

Under No. 5 in the preceding section I noted how I kept missing similar (if not the same) questions as I took various practice exams. As I was taking notes on my mistakes I realized I was being too in-depth and writing out full sentences, instead of just the key concepts. (This is about when I remembered my middle school approach.) One problem with practice exams is that eventually you start to see how the test writer's mind works. Certain words and phrases make repeat appearances, or sentence structure itself gives away an answer. But practice tests are not the real thing, and this can be dangerous, so I didn't want to waste my time focusing on one test that might or might not accurately reflect the exam; better to look at as many tests as possible and just identity key concepts and trigger words.

For instance, one question I missed more than once had to do with risk on schedules, and how after making a network diagram the project manager could identify risks due to converging and diverging activity paths. The key concept is that things *diverging* do not cause risks; things converging do (like cars, for instance). So for me and my brain, that's represented by: Convergent = Risk ≠ Divergent. What I wanted to do was establish a light switch in my brain that flicked on when either the word convergent or divergent was read in conjunction with risk. That mental light would illuminate my basic equation and help me decide on the right answer. For me that's the key: simplify the question.

After taking several practices tests, reading a variety of sources, and noting it all down in various formats, eventually my notes of mistakes and wrong turns evolved into a big list of simple relationships. It might look like gibberish if you haven't dug into the PMP world yet (and if that's the case, well then, hop to it!), so the key to remember is each sequence has a positive relationship unless there is an unequal sign (≠). Read the slashes (/) as: *implies, associated with,* or *has* and the (->) as: *leads to.*

Achievement Theory/ David McClelland/ achievement/ power/ affiliation

Acquire Team ≠ co-location

Activity List ≠ WBS

Activity Definition/ decompose work packages to schedule activities for estimates, schedules, controlling, etc.

ADR/ Alternate Dispute Resolution/ preferred method is negotiation

Cost Aggregation -> schedule activity work package level -> higher WBS levels (control accounts) -> total cost

AOA = Arrow Diagramming Method (ADM)/ dummy/ multiple time estimates/ **only** FS dependency

AON = PDM/ most software uses/ single time estimates/ **can use** 4 dependencies

Approved Change Request -> control

Approved defect repairs -> DMPE -> Implemented defect repairs

Arrow diagram/ Finish to Start (FS)

Assurance -> audit

Benefit measurement methods: comparative/ scoring/ cash flow

Business case/ business need/ investment worthwhile

CEPC: Code of Ethics and Professional Conduct

Closing = formalizing completion/ disseminate information

Code of Accounts/ WBS/ unique identifiers -> chart of accounts -> track costs of work elements

Control Account/ WBS/ EVM calculations

Communication Requirement Analysis/ channels

Common Cause of Variance/ random/ known (predicable)/ always present (inherent)

Compromise/ no winners/ no losers

Configuration Management System/ updated documents/ manage changes and baselines

Configuration Management/ physical characteristics/ functionality

Contingency Theory/ 3Cs: **c**ombination *Theory* Y & *Hygiene*/ **c**onstant **c**ompetency

Contracts

> Cost Reimbursable/ high uncertainty/ big investment before completion
>
> FP Fixed Price/ can include incentives
>
> FFP Firm Fixed Price
>
> CPIF Cost Plus Incentive Fee
>
> CPAF Cost Plus Award Fee/ depending on buyer satisfaction
>
> CPPC Cost Plus % Cost
>
> FP EPA Fixed Price
>
> T&M unknown money/ unknown finish

Corrective action/ future state/ deadline

Cost of Quality/ TT of Estimate Costs

Crashing/ add resources/ speed up

Critical Chain = buffer

Critical Path = highest schedule risk

Defect/ immediate/ past

Direct and Manage Project Execution/ defects/ most difficult part is Integrating

Discretionary dependencies/ arbitrary total float values/ can limit scheduling/ preferred logic, soft logic

DOE Design of Experiments/ multiple changes at once

Duration typically calendar

$EAC - AC = ETC$

Effort typically work hours

Backward Pass/ $LF - Duration + 1 = LS$

Forward Pass/ $ES + Duration - 1 = EF$

Float = Slack = $LS - ES$, if $= 0 =$ critical path activity

$ES = $ prev $EF + 1$

Estimate -> budget -> control

EVM/ WBS/ control account

Expert power/ knowledge and skills

Expectancy Theory/ Victor Vroom/ behavior based on realistic rewards

Fast tracking/ overlapping projects/ iterative phase to phase/ parallel

Force Fields/ drivers/ resistors/ barriers/ enablers

Funding limit reconciliation/ to be spent/ limits

Future ops/maintenance cost = ongoing cost = not project costs

GERT/ loops/ branches/ conditions

High IRR = favored/ preferred

Hygiene Theory/ Frederick Herzberg/ environment (pay, benefits, conditions) prevent dissatisfaction while motivators (challenges, opportunities to improve, advancement) lead to satisfaction

ICC changes the project (the what)

Inspections/ reviews/ audits/ walkthroughs

IRR assumes IRR rate, discount rate NPV = 0

Kick off = phase start

$LF - LS + 1 = D$

Lose Lose/ withdrawal (avoidance) and smoothing (accommodating)

$LS = $ post LS - 1

Mandatory Dependencies/ hard logic

MCPE controls project execution (the how)

No effect to bottom line or end product? No need for CCB

Nominal Group Technique/ brainstorm/ post-it notes risks/ written prioritization/ full risk list

OBS = Organizational Breakdown Structure/ org chart with departments, work units, teams (not individuals)

NPV > 0 = Accept

NPV assumes cost of capital

Parametric/ computer/ multiply/ calculate

Payback Period is *least* precise

Perform Quality Assurance = greatest influence over quality

PERT = (opt + pess + (4 x most likely))/ 6

Physical inspection of work result -> control

Plan Do Check Act/ small changes first

Pareto Charts/ rank-order of importance/ histogram

Run Charts/ variations over time/ trends

PMIS is part of EEF input to Develop Project Management Plan

Portfolio/ strategic business goal

Process Improvement Plan is an output of Plan Quality

Procurement documents/ RFP, RFQ, RFI, IFB/ description of work/ contract SOW/ response submittal method

Procurement Management Plan ≠ Administer Procurements Input

Procurement Negotiations/ can be own process

Product Analysis/ value engineering/ value analysis/ system analysis/ system engineering/ product breakdown/ functional analysis

Product descriptions/ Initiating (less to more later on)

Program/ shared benefit

Progressive Elaboration/ detailed steps/ features of a product

Project Charter/ PM authority/ not detailed

Project Constraints = Scope, Cost, Time, Quality, Risk, Resources

Project Management organizes activities/ tools and techniques

Project Managers manage/ project processes/ stakeholder expectations

Project Success/ stakeholder needs and expectations

Project Time Management: DSEED: **D**efine Activities, **S**equence Activities, **E**stimate Activity Resources, **E**stimate Activity Durations, **D**evelop Schedule *then Control Schedule*

Requirements Document input WBS

Referent power/ respect

RBS = Risk Breakdown Structure OR Resource Breakdown Structure/ track project costs/ tied accounting

RMS/ Records Management System/ part of PMIS

Resource leveling/ split tasks/ under allocated/ delay start

Quality

    Crosby/ zero defects/ prevent defects/ right first time

    Deming/ 85% management problem/ process is problem, not people

    Juran/ fitness for use/ meet or exceed

    Feingenbaum/ father TQM

    Shewhart/ grandfather TQM/ Control Charts/ corrective action applied when process out of control/ Plan Do Check Act/ small changes first

Risk

    Gaps ≠ Risk

    Reserve Analysis/ schedule risk/ add %

    Decision tree/ risk events/ time or cost (EMV)

    Convergent = Risk ≠ Divergent

    Negative/ ATM: accept, transfer, mitigate

    Positive/ SEE: share, enhance, exploit

    Monte Carlo/ schedule risk

    Risk Identification/ lessons learned

    Influence tree/ causal influences among variables

    Risk audits/ implementation and effectiveness risk strategies

    Risk Management Plan ≠ risk responses/ triggers

    Preventative action/ reduce impact negative risks

    Secondary Risk/ new risk because of risk response

    Residual Risk/ leftover risk after risk response

    Watchlist for low priority risks/ don't need risk responses yet

    Unknown Unknown = Management Reserve

    Known Unknown = Contingency

Qualitative/ EMV/ sensitivity analysis/ simulation/ numbers

Quality/ finding defects/ dealing with defects

Quantitative/ probability/ impact/ judgment/ prioritization

Risk Register $\neq$ probability & impact

S Curve/ cost performance baseline

Selected Sellers output requires negotiated contracts

Scope changes are WBS changes and often lead to schedule changes

Scope Management Plan $\neq$ Scope Statement OR Requirements Documents

Scope Planning -> Scope Statement ->Scope Definition -> Create WBS

Scope Statement + WBS + WBS dictionary = Scope Baseline

Scope Statement/ elaborates deliverables/ constraints/ assumptions

Sequence Activities = identify dependencies

Smoothing/ non-permanent/ resurfaces

SOW/ business need/ product scope description/ support strategic plan

Staffing Management Plan/ training/ reward/ recognition/ release

Standard Deviation = (pess – opt) /6; within +/- 1 (68%); +/- 2 (95%); +/- 3 (99%); diversity

Tannenbaum and Schmidt/ 7 levels/ manager authority vs. progressively delegated freedom

Hershey and Blanchard/ Situational Leadership/ directive, coaching, supportive, delegating

Tornado diagram/ uncertain events at baseline values

TABRT

Weak matrix/ less stress

Win Lose/ forcing

Work Authorization System/ company defined

Work Performance Information $\neq$ defects

WPI -> WP Measurements -> forecasts (EAC, ETC, etc.) -> Performance Reports

X $\neq$ trust = Y/ proper motivation and expectations

Z = loyalty/ life

So that's my personal list of test mistakes. Yours will probably be different. The key is to take notes of what you missed to realize *how* you will remember *what* about each mistake so you can avoid repeating it. Hopefully you read that list and saw some relationships to the diagrams I used in the beginning. If not, don't worry. You don't have to use what I used. This is just an example of how I did it. Anybody can adapt the *how* so don't fight your nature. Just stop and think and realize what triggers and relationships work in *your* brain to help *your* memory work. Then just keep practicing and stay in the zone.

Obviously, you're already at the stage of preparing to take the test, so you probably fall into one of these categories:

1. Your boss said to take it
2. You're trying to get a new job
3. You want to stay competitive in your existing job market

The counterargument to getting your PMP is that it's just a certification and who cares if you have another piece of paper framed on your wall? A good project manager doesn't need a certification because a reputation speaks for itself. When you're good, people know you're good, and they aren't asking for a reference. Of course, that argument only holds for the third reason up there. The first one is a no-brainer. The second reason is like a pillow in the zombie apocalypse: y'know, I'd rather have it and not need it than the other way around. If something *might* help and by not having it you *might* be at a disadvantage, well then, there you go. The real question isn't if the PMP is useful. Of course, it's useful. All certifications are useful. The real question is one of value.

I paid for the PMP myself because I think it's worth a couple of hundred bucks. My boss thinks it's worthless so he wasn't gonna pay. My job doesn't require it. Actually, opinion is pretty evenly split within the world of government software development whether a PM needs this certification or not. In the highway construction industry, where I spent the first seven years of my career, I'd never even heard of it. Ultimately, it's a very strenuous test that people who pass feel themselves part of a select group while people who haven't taken it don't care about it at all, or just think it's a colossal waste of time, effort, and money. I certainly *don't* think it's worth a couple of thousand dollars. My reviews of PMP boot camps were spotty at best so I wasn't willing to bet on one being good enough to get me what I needed. Not when the library is free and the internet is at my fingertips.

So do I use my PMP? Yeah, I do use some of it. Depending on a project's needs and because I studied like hell to pass, occasionally I dredge up something of immediate value. Usually someone else makes a PMP reference and I'm not lost listening to them. I found studying the material interesting at the very least. It did round out my general knowledge of project management, most of which was learned on the fly as I came up through the ranks, and served to organize the information.

A friend of mine told me his theory was to take any and all training or certifications offered by his company. His reasoning was that he didn't care what it was; if someone else in the industry thought it was important enough to have a class about he wanted to be able to measure his success by their standards. As an added bonus it shows that you are a team player. But again, *value* is the key idea here: if someone else is paying, sure I'll take it. But if I'm paying I have to reason it out for myself if it's worthwhile or not. So half the people in government think the PMP doesn't matter. Then by having it I'm not really changing their opinion: it doesn't matter to them. But that other half *do* think it's worth *something*, and that matters to *me*.

www.ingramcontent.com/pod-product-compliance
Lightning Source LLC
Chambersburg PA
CBHW051303170526

45165CB00004B/1837